Tough, Toothy

BABY SHARKS

Sandra Markle

Walker & Company   New York

You may not have seen a baby shark before. This is a baby Brown-Banded Bamboo Shark. It will grow up in the shallow waters off coral reefs along the coast of India and islands as far south as northern Australia. But there are lots of different kinds of sharks in all of the world's oceans. Some can even be found in fresh-water rivers and lakes. And wherever they live, sharks produce babies. So how is a baby shark born? How does it live and stay safe? And what kinds of changes happen as it grows up? This book will let you take a close look at baby sharks—those animals nicknamed shark "pups."

THEY'RE FISH

Sharks are fish, but they belong to a group of animals called *Chondrichthyes* (kon-DRIK-thees). That means they are a kind of fish whose skeletons are made of lightweight, rubbery *cartilage* (KAR-tel-ij) instead of bone. To know what cartilage is like, feel your ear. Its strong but flexible shape comes from a cartilage framework.

Sharks, like this Great White, are different in other ways from bony fish such as the Skipjack Tuna it's eating. For example, a shark's *gills*, the special body parts that carry *oxygen* from the water into the body, are in separate pouches, each with a slit opening to the outside. Bony fish, on the other hand, have gills grouped together in one chamber under a protective cover. If you could peek inside, you'd discover another important difference. Bony fish have what looks like a balloon, called a swim bladder or a gas bladder. Sharks lack this. By gulping in air or burping it out, bony fish help themselves float up or sink. Sharks have to swim to keep from sinking. However, they get a little help from their huge liver. This is packed with lightweight oils, making their bodies somewhat buoyant.

Starting Life in an Egg

Sharks also reproduce differently than bony fish do. These Port Jackson Sharks are mating. Most female bony fish produce hundreds—even thousands—of tiny *eggs* and release them into the water. Next, their mates release their reproductive cells, called *sperm*, over the eggs. Then the eggs and sperm merge, or the eggs become fertilized, outside the female's body. In sharks, however, fertilization happens inside the female's body. Some female sharks may produce as many as seventy or eighty eggs to be fertilized, but none produce very large numbers of eggs. Many, like Port Jackson Sharks, produce only a few.

As with most kinds of sharks, the female Port Jackson Shark is larger than the male. She has to be in order for her body to hold the large eggs she'll produce. She also needs to be bigger to catch and eat enough prey to supply the food energy she needs to produce eggs. The male is biting the female to hold on to her. He has a stiff, grooved, tubelike extension on each of his two pelvic fins. Inserting one or the other of these, he deposits his sperm into her reproductive tract.

Inside, female sharks have a special body part called a *shell gland*, where the sperm cells usually fertilize, or unite with, the egg cells. In some types of sharks, like Port Jackson Sharks, the shell gland also coats the fertilized egg with a protective case. Then this case with the enclosed developing young is called the egg.

The Port Jackson Shark's egg is about 3 inches (8 centimeters) wide and 5 inches (13 centimeters) long. The tough, leathery egg case is soft at first. After the egg leaves the mother's body, she picks it up in her mouth and pushes it into a crack in the rocks. There the case hardens. Its coloring helps hide it. But even if a predator does spot the shark's egg, the egg's spiral shape—now locked into the rock crack—usually keeps it safe.

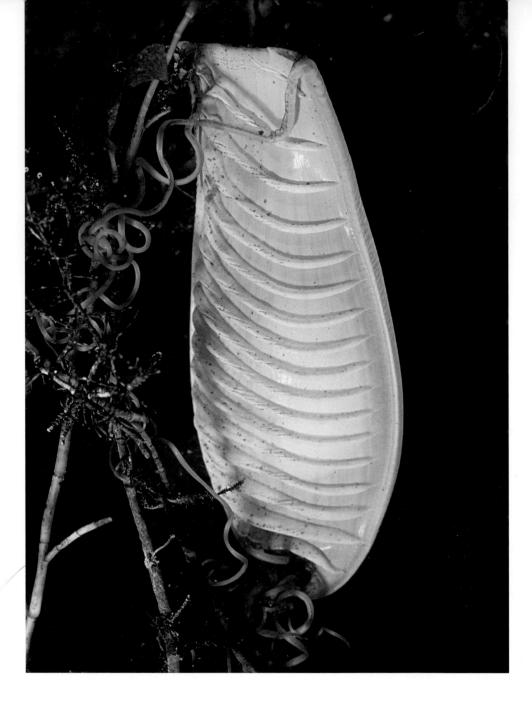

Draftboard Swell Sharks lay eggs too. Their egg cases have threadlike tendrils at each corner. As the egg leaves the female's body, she swims close to coral, seaweed, or rocks. Then the tendrils catch and wrap tight, anchoring the egg.

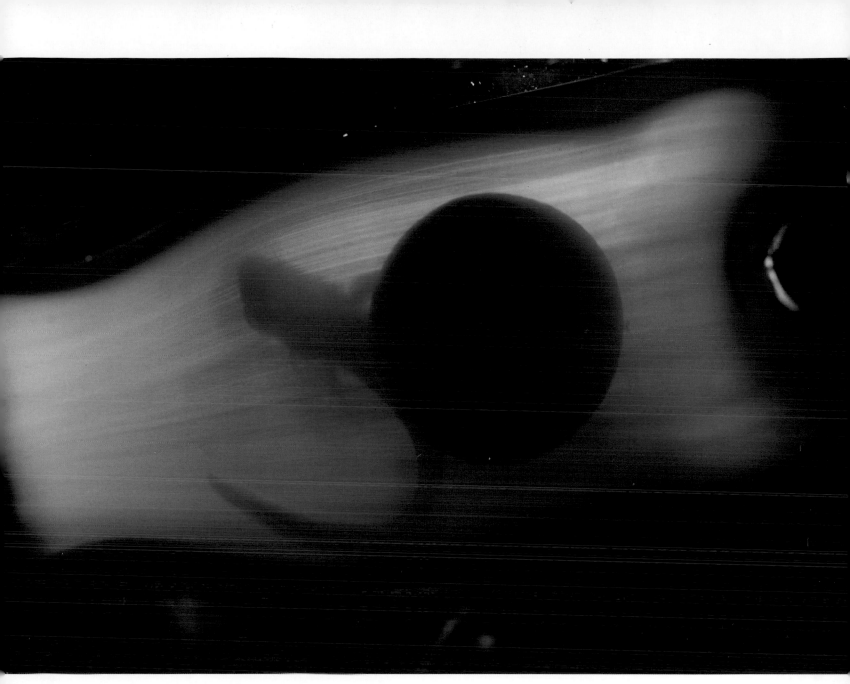

Safe inside its egg, this baby Draftboard Swell Shark develops. It's attached to its food source, a ball of fat and protein called the *yolk*. As this food is absorbed, the yolk ball shrinks. This way, it provides the pup with both the energy and the space it needs to grow.

Finally, after nearly twelve months of developing, the baby is about 5 inches (13 centimeters) long and ready to hatch out of its egg.

Another difference between sharks and bony fish is their protective body covering. Look at the head of a Shadowfin Soldier Fish (left) to see that its scales, like those of most bony fish, are shield-shaped plates.

Then take a close look at the head of a Port Jackson Shark (right). A shark's scales, called *denticles* (DEN-ti-kelz), are like little teeth, complete with enamel.

When it's ready to hatch, the baby Draftboard Swell Shark develops two rows of larger, rear-pointing denticles down the length of its back. These catch and rip open the egg case so the baby can escape. They also keep the baby from sliding back into its egg while it's struggling to exit. The pup soon sheds these special denticles. Throughout its life, it will regularly shed and replace all its denticles.

SAFE INSIDE

This female Tawny Nurse Shark's belly is bulging because about forty baby sharks are inside. Some shark mothers keep the fertilized eggs inside two special parts of the reproductive tract, the *uteri* (YUU-teh-rye). But the mother's body doesn't do much more than house the growing babies. During the nearly five months it takes each baby Tawny Nurse Shark to develop, it is curled up inside its own tennis ball–size egg, living off its attached yolk ball. Luckily, the female Tawny Nurse Shark is a big mama, more than 9 feet (3 meters) long. By the time her brood is fully developed and hatches, each of the pups is about 15 inches (38 centimeters) long and weighs about 1 pound (0.5 kilogram).

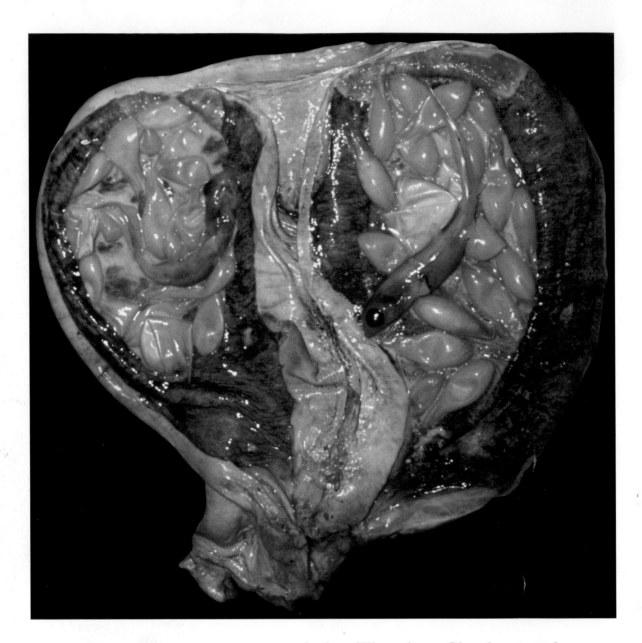

Here you can see two baby Thresher Sharks inside their mother's uteri. Unlike Tawny Nurse Sharks, baby Threshers need more time to develop after they use up their own yolk supply. So, the female's body keeps producing unfertilized eggs, which move into the uteri. After the pups hatch, they remain inside their mother, eating unfertilized eggs while they continue growing.

By the time they're fully developed, each Thresher Shark pup is about 3 feet (0.9 meter) long. Nearly half of that length is tail. Once on their own, the pups will use their long tails like whips to herd *schools*, or groups, of herring and other fish closer together, making their prey easier to catch.

PUP RIVALRY

Inside this female Sandtiger Shark, there's a contest going on. Sandtiger pups also hatch inside their mother, but they eat more than the unfertilized eggs. They eat their brothers and sisters!

Some of the female's eggs become fertilized. The pups that hatch are, at first, no bigger than your little finger. However, they quickly develop a set of fanglike teeth. Then the hungry pups become extremely active, snapping at everything they come across. They devour any unfertilized eggs, and the bigger pups eat any smaller pups they can catch. This gives the bigger pups energy to grow even bigger. It also gives them more room to grow. After about nine months, only two pups remain—the biggest and strongest pup in each of the female's two uteri. At birth, each of these pups will be a little more than 3 feet (0.9 meter) long—about a third of its mother's length.

TAKING CARE OF BABY

This newborn Lemon Shark pup is just swimming away from its mother. Baby Lemon Sharks also develop inside their mothers, but they get the food they need in a different way. After a few months, when the yolk supply is used up, the yolk sac develops lots of blood vessels and folds that make the tissue look wrinkled. Like putting your hands together with intertwined fingers, these folds match up with similar wrinkles in the lining of the mother's uterus. This allows blood vessels in the yolk sac to come in contact with blood vessels in the uterus. Then dissolved food nutrients in the mother's blood pass through the vessel walls into the pup's blood. Chemical wastes go in the opposite direction.

After developing for a little more than a year, this Lemon Shark pup slipped out of its mother's body tail-first. Now, after resting for a few minutes, it's swimming away, pulling with it the remains of the yolk sac and breaking the connecting cord. Soon, one at a time, the pup's fourteen brothers and sisters will be born the same way.

An Ocean Nursery

Like all sharks, the Lemon Shark pups are on their own from birth. Before they were born, their mother swam into a warm, shallow lagoon full of mangrove trees. So the pups start life in a relatively safe nursery. Just 2 feet (0.6 meter) long, the newborns can easily swim among the mangrove trees' roots. There they hunt for fish, stingrays, crabs, and crayfish during the day, and they hide from the larger sharks that come into the lagoon to hunt at night. They remain in their nursery lagoon for several years, slowly expanding their hunting range into deeper water as they grow bigger.

SAFE IN SCHOOL

Like Lemon Shark pups, this Hammerhead pup received food from its mother through a yolk sac prior to birth. Now it's on its own in the shallow bay that is its nursery. Many Hammerhead females swim to this bay each summer to give birth. Some have as few as twelve pups. This pup had thirty-one siblings!

Only about 18 inches (46 centimeters) long at birth, Hammerhead pups find safety in ganging together into a school. Although adult Hammerheads may travel alone or in large schools, hundreds of pups may school together. The school avoids larger predators by staying in shallow water during the day. The pups venture into deeper water only at night, when bigger sharks are less likely to spot them. Then they hunt for bony fish like barracuda.

BECOMING AN ADULT

While some baby sharks are like miniature versions of their parents, others are different. For example, Scalloped Hammerheads have a more distinctly scalloped head as babies. And Nurse Shark youngsters have dark spots all over their bodies that disappear as they mature. Compare this older juvenile with the baby on page two to see what happens to the Brown-Banded Bamboo Shark's stripes as it grows up. They fade!

Baby Port Jackson Sharks like this one change their teeth and what they eat as they mature. As babies they have a mouthful of mainly pointed teeth and most often eat soft-bodied fish. As they mature, broad, flat teeth replace their pointed back teeth. Then they switch to crushing and eating sea urchins and hard-shelled mollusks like clams.

Young sharks become mature adults once they're able to mate and produce young of their own. Reaching that stage, though, is more a matter of size than age. For example, this Whitetip Reef Shark will be mature once it grows to be about 4 feet (1.2 meters) long—about double its birth length. How big a shark has to be in order to be mature varies with the kind of shark. But to become an adult, baby sharks have to obtain plenty of food energy. So, wherever there are shark pups in the world's oceans, rivers, and lakes, they're hunting in order to grow up.

Where in the World Are These Sharks?

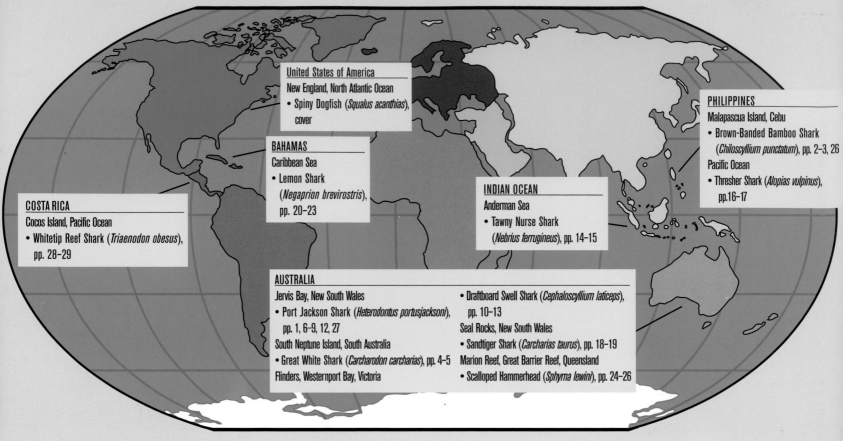

United States of America
New England, North Atlantic Ocean
- Spiny Dogfish (*Squalus acanthias*), cover

BAHAMAS
Caribbean Sea
- Lemon Shark (*Negaprion brevirostris*), pp. 20–23

COSTA RICA
Cocos Island, Pacific Ocean
- Whitetip Reef Shark (*Triaenodon obesus*), pp. 28–29

INDIAN OCEAN
Anderman Sea
- Tawny Nurse Shark (*Nebrius ferrugineus*), pp. 14–15

PHILIPPINES
Malapascua Island, Cebu
- Brown-Banded Bamboo Shark (*Chiloscyllium punctatum*), pp. 2–3, 26
Pacific Ocean
- Thresher Shark (*Alopias vulpinus*), pp.16–17

AUSTRALIA
Jervis Bay, New South Wales
- Port Jackson Shark (*Heterodontus portusjacksoni*), pp. 1, 6–9, 12, 27
South Neptune Island, South Australia
- Great White Shark (*Carcharodon carcharias*), pp. 4–5
Flinders, Westernport Bay, Victoria
- Draftboard Swell Shark (*Cephaloscyllium laticeps*), pp. 10–13
Seal Rocks, New South Wales
- Sandtiger Shark (*Carcharias taurus*), pp. 18–19
Marion Reef, Great Barrier Reef, Queensland
- Scalloped Hammerhead (*Sphyrna lewini*), pp. 24–26

While the sharks you discovered in this book may also be found in other parts of the world, check the map to see where they were photographed. The page numbers let you know where to find them in the book.

S.O.S.
(Save Our Sharks)

Many sharks, like the Great White, are among the ocean's top predators. As such, they play an important role in controlling the populations of prey species, like barracuda, and keeping marine ecosystems balanced. While shark attacks on humans make the news, such attacks are rare. On the other hand, every year, people kill many sharks for sport, for food, or because their parts are wrongly believed to cure diseases. Conservationists are working to protect sharks, but about seventy-five different kinds of sharks are in danger of becoming extinct. The fact that many sharks are being killed is an especially big problem because most produce only a small number of babies in their lifetime. How can you help? Work with your family to avoid purchasing any products made from sharks. If you live near the ocean, work with your community to help prevent pollution. That helps all of the animals in marine ecosystems, including sharks.

Sharks Are Cool!

Biggest! Littlest! The largest kind of shark is the Whale Shark, which, as an adult, grows to be as long as 46 feet (14 meters). The smallest is the Dwarf Lantern Shark, which grows to be only about 5 inches (13 centimeters) long.

Shark Tooth Fairy Sharks lose teeth throughout their life—not just as pups. That's because most sharks have a mouth full of rows of teeth, but they usually bite and tear their food with only the front few rows. As teeth become worn or broken, they fall out and replacement teeth move forward.

Swim and Taste Besides being able to taste with sensors in their mouths, sharks have taste-sensitive spots all over their bodies. So, in a way, sharks are tasting the water as they swim. This helps them find and track prey.

Super Sniffer Most sharks have nostrils, but they don't breathe through these. Swimming forces water through a shark's nostrils, into its nasal sacs. There, chemical particles in the water are detected and the shark "smells" scents like blood, which can mean wounded and easier-to-catch prey.

GLOSSARY/INDEX

CARTILAGE [KAR-tel-ij] Lightweight, strong, rubbery connective tissue that forms a shark's skeleton instead of bone. 4

DENTICLES [DEN-ti-kelz] Teethlike scales covering a shark's body. 12, 13

EGG [eg] The name given to the female reproductive cell. It is also the name given to the fertilized egg that will produce a baby shark. 7, 8, 10–13, 14, 16, 19

GILL [gil] The body part in which oxygen is extracted from the water. 4

OXYGEN [AHK-sih-jen] A gas in the air and water that passes into the blood in the gills. The blood then carries it through the body, where it is combined with food to release energy. 4

SCHOOL [skool] A group of fish that stays together in order to keep safe and have an easier time catching food. 17, 24, 25

SHELL GLAND [shel gland] Special body part in the female where the male's sperm usually unites with the eggs. In some kinds of sharks, it also coats the fertilized egg with a protective case. 8

SPERM [spurm] The male reproductive cell. When the sperm joins with the female's egg cell, a baby shark develops. 7, 8

UTERI [YUU-teh-rye] The paired part of the female's body where eggs are contained and, in some cases, the young develop. 14, 16, 19

YOLK [yohk] Food supply for developing young. 11, 14, 16, 20, 24

With love for Genista Friesen

Tough, Toothy Baby Sharks was inspired by an awesome experience I had. I swam with sharks! I love snorkeling, and on one occasion while watching colorful reef fish and stingrays in Moorea, French Polynesia, I suddenly saw several Whitetip Reef Sharks cruising through the water beneath me. They stayed well away from me and the other human swimmers as they pursued a fish dinner. I was impressed with these graceful, effective ocean predators and wanted to learn more about their lives. This fascination led me to search for and get to know shark experts and photographers around the world. Take another look at the photos in *Tough, Toothy Baby Sharks* and you'll share a unique peek at young sharks taken by people who went to great effort to work underwater studying and photographing them.

First published in the United States of America in 2007 by Walker Publishing Company, Inc.
Distributed to the trade by Holtzbrinck Publishers

For information about permission to reproduce selections from this book, write to Permissions, Walker & Company, 104 Fifth Avenue, New York, New York 10011

Library of Congress Cataloging-in-Publication Data
Markle, Sandra.
Tough, toothy baby sharks / by Sandra Markle.
p.   cm.
ISBN-13: 978-0-8027-9593-9 • ISBN-10: 0-8027-9593-5 (hardcover)
ISBN-13: 978-0-8027-9594-6 • ISBN-10: 0-8027-9594-3 (reinforced)
1. Sharks—Infancy—Juvenile literature. I. Title.
QL638.9.M284 2007   597.3—dc22   2006101178

Book design by Nicole Gastonguay

Visit Walker & Company's Web site at www.walkeryoungreaders.com

Printed in China
10 9 8 7 6 5 4 3 2 1 (hardcover)
10 9 8 7 6 5 4 3 2 1 (reinforced)

Acknowledgments:
I would especially like to thank Dr. Harold "Wes" Pratt, Coordinator of Keys Shark Research, Mote Marine Laboratory; and Dr. Samuel "Doc" Gruber, Director of the Bimini Biological Field Station of Rosenstiel School of Marine and Atmospheric Science at the University of Miami, for sharing their expertise and enthusiasm. A special thank-you to Skip Jeffery for his help and support throughout the creative process.

Photo Credits:
Francis Abbott—Nature Picture Library 15
Kelvin Aitken—Marine Themes 1, 2, 9, 10, 12b, 27
Mark Conlin—Marine Themes 5, 11, 13
David Harasti—Marine Themes 6
Richard Hermann—Marine Themes cover
Skip Jeffery 30
Jim Knowlton—SeaPics 23
Mary Malloy—Marine Themes 18
Doug Perrine—Nature Picture Library 17, 26
Wes Pratt 16
Jeff Rotman 21, 24, 29
Tony Wu—Marine Themes 12a, 25